Rani Comes to Stay

Story by Jackie Tidey
Photography by Lindsay Edwards

W9-ASU-627

Rigby
A Harcourt Achieve Imprint

www.Rigby.com
1-800-531-5015

"Hello, Rani," said Meg's mom.

"Please come in."

Rani said goodbye
to her mother.

Rani said to Meg,
"My mom is going away
to see Grandma."

"Yes," said Meg,
"and you are going
to stay with us."

The girls went into Meg's room.

"Where am I going to sleep?"
said Rani.

"You are going to sleep
in this little bed,"
said Meg.

After dinner
the girls went to bed.

They read some books.

Meg looked at Rani.

"Mom," said Meg,
"come and see Rani.
She is crying."

Mom came in to see the girls.

"Can I please go home?"
said Rani.

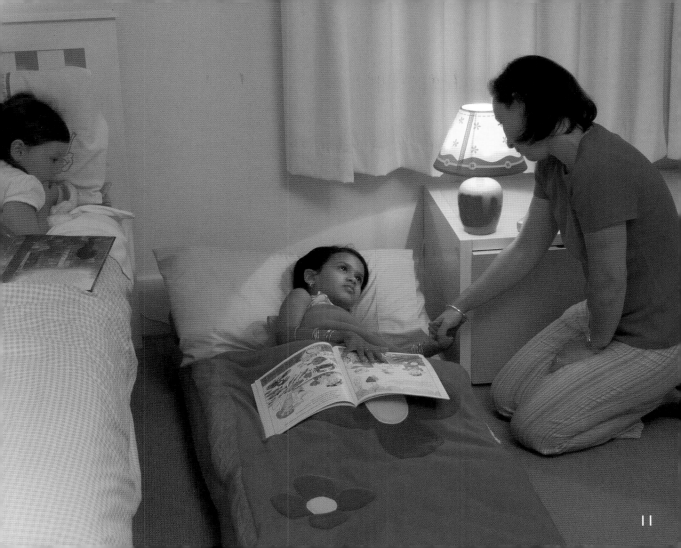

"Rani," said Meg's mom,
"we will look after you.
Your mother is coming back
to get you after breakfast."

Meg said,
"Here is my little rabbit, Rani."

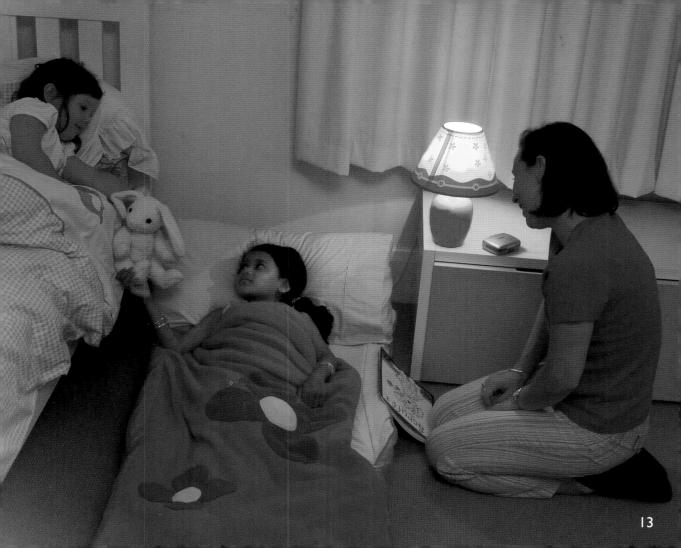

"Thank you, Meg," said Rani.
"I like your rabbit."

Meg's mom said,
"Go to sleep, girls.
I will stay here with you."

And the girls went to sleep.